This Is My Office
and
Notes on My Mother's Decline

This Is My Office
and
Notes on My Mother's Decline TWO PLAYS

ANDY BRAGEN

Foreword by Sarah Ruhl

NORTHWESTERN UNIVERSITY PRESS

EVANSTON, ILLINOIS

Northwestern University Press
www.nupress.northwestern.edu

Cover at top and page 1: David Barlow on the set of *This Is My Office*, November 2013. Photographs by Fitz Patton.

Cover at bottom: Caroline Lagerfelt on the set of *Notes on My Mother's Decline*, and page 35: Caroline Lagerfelt and Ari Fliakos on set, November 2019. Photographs by Marsha Ginsberg.

Poems cited on pages 61–62 and 83 are from *Japanese Death Poems: Written by Zen Monks and Haiku Poets on the Verge of Death*, compiled by and with an introduction by Yoel Hoffmann (Tokyo, Rutland, VT, and Singapore: Tuttle Publishing, 1985).

Printed in the United States of America

10 9 8 7 6 5 4 3 2 1

LIBRARY OF CONGRESS
CATALOGING-IN-PUBLICATION DATA

Names: Bragen, Andy, author. | Bragen, Andy. This is my office. | Bragen, Andy. Notes on my mother's decline.
Title: This is my office ; and, Notes on my mother's decline : two plays / Andy Bragen.
Description: Evanston : Northwestern University Press, 2022.
Identifiers: LCCN 2021039783 | ISBN 9780810144613 (paperback) | ISBN 9780810144620 (ebook)
Classification: LCC PS3602.R344418 T48 2022 | DDC 812.6—dc23
LC record available at https://lccn.loc .gov/2021039783

For my parents

CONTENTS

FOREWORD

Sarah Ruhl

One of my favorite endings of a play is from *This Is My Office*. The final page begins with something of a list poem, Sei Shōnagon style, in which the speaker tells us he's made a list of things he loved about his late father:

> his handkerchiefs (I use them now)
> the pizza we ate together (at the Orchidia and elsewhere)
> his glasses (quite thick)
> his comb-over
> his hat
> his voice
> his handwriting (worse than mine) . . .
> his puzzles
> his books
> his mind
> his ears (they grew)
> his teeth (false, I threw them away)
> his nose
> his lips (dry toward the end)
> his eyes (tired)
> his love.
> Oh God. His love.

The speaker goes on to invite us all to meet the cast and mingle after the play, reminding us that we are, in fact, in the theater together; there is no proscenium dividing us, not really. If anything this is a ritual, and there is room here for all of our grief. And then the play ends:

One last memory. That of my father, remembering his father. He told me this story on our drive back to Secaucus from the oncologist, right after he'd been given the death sentence. It was 1974, the summer of my first birthday. His father, David Bragen, in his late sixties at the time, came to Britain to visit my parents, who'd rented a cottage there for August. David had had a couple of strokes, and was nearly blind. He wanted to hold me, and he held me in his arms. So here we are, my dad and I, driving on the turnpike. I joked, "It's a wonder he didn't drop me." My father didn't hesitate: "He would never drop you," he said. "He would never let that happen." Thank you.

I remember watching that last moment in the theater (which in the New York production moved into an installation of a bedroom similar to the one where the playwright's father really died, in Secaucus, New Jersey). We abandon the sad anonymous office space—looking for a ghost. It's Christmas Eve, a time for ghosts. When we entered the bedroom, I lost it, holding a business card that we had been handed out, with the playwright's father's name on it: Harold Bragen. I thought about my own father, whom I'd lost too young. And I thought about Harold, and I was wracked with the most embarrassing sobs. I knew Harold because I know the playwright, Andy Bragen, quite well. And it was difficult to separate the art of the play from the life I knew that was now missing. Part of the play's purpose, it seems to me, is to blur the line between art and life, to reject artifice in favor of theater's extraordinary potential for intimacy and tenderness.

Both of the plays in this volume are highly contemporary, personal containers for grief that is as ancient as *Oedipus*. Both of these plays invite the audience to participate in a ritual for grief that is seasoned with the contemporary mundane, looking for an ancient portal to howl through. The plays are coupled—both revelations of how the theater can accommodate authentic grief and personhood.

I met Andy Bragen when we were in our early twenties and both taking a playwriting class in Taxco, Mexico, with María Irene Fornés. We became fast friends and have been one another's literary protectors ever since. Andy was my guide in New York when I first moved to the city from the Midwest (all of his plays are full of the love of New York in all of its particularity). Andy and I followed Tina Howe around, went to see every inexpensive play we could sneak into, traded pages, and have profoundly watched and participated in each other's writing lives and family lives over the years. I mention this because these plays are too personal not to mention my personal connection to the author. There is nothing academic about my relationship to these plays—I watched them get written, I watched them be born into performance, and I watched their protagonists die in real time.

The second protagonist being Tracy Bragen, Andy's mom. *Notes on My Mother's Decline* follows a mother and son as the mother descends into a bedridden state. Unlike *This Is My Office*, which is written for one speaker, *Notes on My Mother's Decline* is what I'd describe as a duet, the musicality of both plays being very important. The mother and son in *Notes* are so embroiled that for much of the play they aren't even afforded the boundary of character names to distinguish them. The son is so self-protective that he can't be in dialogue with the mother until the very end of the play; before then, the son is almost omniscient, narrating every move his mother (who lives a block away) makes.

At the end, we hear this conversation:

SON
Do you want to hear about it? Your actual death?

MOTHER
I died?

SON
December 16, 2017.

MOTHER
Oh. Darn.

SON
Yeah. I'm sorry.

MOTHER
What happened?

SON
You fell. And had a stroke. You were on the floor by your bed for a little while—we don't know how long—before you managed to pull the phone down to yourself and call Marco, around one in the morning.

MOTHER
Who's Marco?

SON
Marco is David. I've been calling him that. To protect him.

MOTHER
That's stupid.

SON
Your left side was nearly frozen. You couldn't really swallow, couldn't get enough nourishment. We gave you crushed ice chips, and tiny sips of water. The new aide, Monica, would mix Ensure and vanilla ice cream and feed it to you with a spoon. She took amazing care of you.

MOTHER

I loved Monica.

SON

She was so good with you. She was able to understand what you needed, which wasn't easy. After the stroke you were very garbled.

MOTHER

Could you understand me?

SON

Sometimes. I got better at it. You found a way to make yourself understood, by all of us.

MOTHER

That's good.

SON

It was day by day. At times we thought you might be swallowing more, getting better. I was exhausted, not sleeping much. There was a day, not long before the end, where I was totally burnt out. And Monica said to you: "Give Andy a break, let him be with his family." And so I left. But as soon as Monica had left for the day, you had the late-afternoon aide start calling. I said that I'd be there in the morning, but then you had the night aide call, and you made her hold the phone up to your face so you could talk to me. You were begging me to come over.

MOTHER

I wanted to see you. I was dying.

I fear I am quoting far too much of the plays you are about to read; after all, hallelujah, now they are in print and you can hold them in your hands—these beautiful contemporary Noh plays full of ghosts, these arias of loss, these gift plays. Andy told me he wrote the plays as gifts for his parents, for the audience, and, lastly, for himself; though he says when he wrote them, he didn't know how much he needed them.

These plays are searingly honest and tender, honoring real people without the usual claptrap and artifice in what we often call realism. In a sense, Andy has invented a new form in these two plays, what I might call a kind of death-mask play. Don't worry, though, if you feel you might be felled by the macabre—there is plenty of compassion and humor here that will get you through the long night. After the pandemic we've all been through, we need tenderness from our theater, a container for our grief, and an acknowledgment of the human life that animates the work. You will find all of that in these pages. I am grateful for these plays, as I am grateful for the writer who wrote them.

ACKNOWLEDGMENTS

The road to production and publication is long and winding, and I am grateful to the many friends and colleagues who have supported this journey. Before its premiere, *This Is My Office* received terrific workshop productions in Rhode Island and Virginia, thanks to Lowry Marshall at Brown/Trinity Playwrights Rep and Kenley Smith and Todd Ristau at Studio Roanoke. Along the way, there were numerous readings of both of these plays, many at New Dramatists, where I was a resident playwright from 2012 to 2019. I am grateful to their entire staff, in particular Emily Morse and John Steber, for all of their wisdom, warmth, and goodwill over the years. I wrote *This Is My Office* while on a Workspace Residency with the Lower Manhattan Cultural Council and developed *Notes on My Mother's Decline* while on another LMCC residency on Governor's Island. Thank you, LMCC, for providing me with space and time.   ·

Notes on My Mother's Decline wouldn't be half the play it is without the wisdom and kindness of the original members of my writing group, the Pickle Council: Jorge Ignacio Cortiñas, Sarah Ruhl, and Kathleen Tolan. I admire all of them so much. Sarah has been a warm, wise, and generous friend and colleague for decades—I can't thank her enough for the book's lovely foreword and for all that she has done for me over the years. Davis McCallum and Knud Adams directed these plays with rigor, precision, and enormous heart. I couldn't have asked for better productions, and the bulk of the credit goes to them, and to the terrific designers they brought on. Thank you especially to the actors in these productions: David Barlow, Ari Fliakos, and Caroline Lagerfelt—these performers brought their own hearts and souls to the roles, and also approached these very personal stories of mine with generosity, love, and enormous craft. I am likewise deeply grateful to The Play Company, which expertly produced these plays. It has been an honor and a privilege to work with so many on their team, including Robert G. Bradshaw, Melissa Hardy, Lauren Weigel, and above all Founding Producer Kate Loewald, who is a fierce advocate for artists and art.

Notes on My Mother's Decline was coproduced by my own company: Andy Bragen Theatre Projects. So many friends and colleagues have supported ABTP over the years, too many to thank everyone individually, but I do want to acknowledge a few steadfast patrons, in particular Rob and Stacey Goergen, Jeffrey Steinman and Jody Falco, Robin Lynn, Joyce Barrett, Jay Flynn and Vicky Cleave, Noel and Tanya Silverman, Evan Silverman, Jeffrey Pruzan, and Bradley Schiff.

This collection is dedicated to my parents, Harold Bragen and Eugenia Mae Moseley Bragen, who taught me to love words and language. I miss them and am forever grateful for all that they gave me.

My wife, Crystal Finn, has been beside me for both of these plays and so much more. Her wisdom, kindness, and love have carried me through. The plays I dedicate to my parents, but my life and my heart belong to her, and to our daughter Delphina.

This Is My Office

A NOTE ON THE PLAY

This Is My Office is meant to be a kind of magic trick. Like the work of Spalding Gray or W. David Hancock, what at first seems simple is meant to open up in a theatrical manner. "Andy," the main character, thinks he's telling one story but falls into another. He loses track, and then "rights himself," only to lose track again. He is an unreliable narrator both for the audience and for himself. He is also very conscious of the audience and their experience, constantly checking in with them. That connection, as in all solo shows, is paramount. I would encourage directors to push toward simple yet bold design choices. In the Providence production, done in the round, the set consisted of a rolling desk chair, a Polaroid photo, a handkerchief, and business cards. I could envision another version wherein the space transforms completely at the end, so that what has been imagined is rendered literally. Might the set likewise be unreliable? Might it also create a kind of magic?

This Is My Office was originally produced for the stage in New York City by The Play Company (Kate Loewald, Founding Producer; Lauren Weigel, Executive Producer) in November 2013. The cast was as follows:

Andy. . . . . David Barlow

The production was directed by Davis McCallum, the set design was by Andrew Boyce, the costume design was by Kaye Voyce, the lighting design was by Tyler Micoleau, the sound design was by Peter John Still, and the stage manager was David Beller.

Performance note: This piece is written for an actor playing a character named Andy Bragen. This device will be acknowledged in the play, and as such the actor does not need to look like the author Andy Bragen or even be Andy's age (thirty-eight at the time of writing).

Welcome. I'm Andy Bragen. This is my office. Well, my literal actual office is over there, see there's my name on the door, but you get the idea. I'm in this space thanks to the Lower Manhattan Cultural Council. They bring arts downtown, down here to the Wall Street district, filling it with cultural events, exhibitions, performances of all sorts, and artists. Like me and my friends here. We get studios, which is to say offices, for nine months, to do whatever the hell we want to do in. Which is exactly what I'm doing. I come here most weekdays, generally during business hours. And while I'm here, I read periodicals online, check my email, and update my Facebook page. I pace back and forth, take regular bathroom breaks and tea breaks, and sometimes go out for coffee, or lunch. Pretty much what everyone does at any office, right? Or so I'm told. Truth is, I've never really worked in an office before, aside from a home office. So office culture, or rather non-home-office culture, is somewhat foreign to me.

Not that we have that here. I mean, technically we're in an office, though in reality it's more precisely the memory of an office, a palimpsest of previous commerce. But even if the space is abandoned, it still has that office feel. Just pay attention to the details; it's all right in front of you. The neutral carpeting, so easy to vacuum and maintain. The wide-open space in the middle where the cubicles were. The kitchenette. The stockroom (I love stockrooms). The modular conference rooms, with space for hanging coats, projecting transparencies, and laying out snack trays. The private windowed offices for the mid-level executives, and of course the corner office, with the East River view and its own executive bathroom. Some bigwig was in there for sure. Never fear, I'll take you there in a little while.

It is weird to be in an office that's no longer an office. When I get here in the morning, and take the elevator up, when I come through what used to be the office suite's side door to this empty area with the red plastic table and a few half-broken rolling chairs, I feel as if I've entered a different world. It feels, as my fellow resident Alicia put it, kind of like a spaceship on a decades-long journey. I'm in this hermetically sealed place, this office that's no longer serving its original purpose, an office that, thanks to a large corporation's generosity and desire (I presume) for a tax write-off, is free. An office that's not producing material for the market, that's decidedly not commercial. Then again, I am easily the most commercial writer in this space at the moment. You may not believe it after you've heard this piece, but I actually get paid for my work sometimes. The other residents are poets mostly, and we know what that's like.

But I do love offices, and always have, love the idea of having my very own fully dedicated work domain. So back in July when I found out I was chosen for this residency, I was over the moon. What an opportunity, I thought! I'll finally be able to get myself out of the house. I'll go to work, every day, just like a real-life businessman. I'll write three plays, two screenplays, and even a libretto, and come next May, when the residency's over, I'll be on top of the world! It hasn't worked out that way. Not due to a lack of ideas, I assure you. I'm full of them, always have been, have never lacked material. Nor due to a lack of commitment: like I said, I'm here every day.

And so it started. I'd leave home for work first thing in the morning, riding the M15 bus down Allen Street, across Madison to St. James Place, then down Water all the way to Maiden Lane. During my first few days here, I spent hours wandering all across the floor, familiarizing myself with every nook and cranny, just like a cat or a dog in its new home. That isn't my typical modus operandi, usually I'm unconcerned with my surroundings, preferring to simply plunge right into work, but something about this space demanded my attention.

It was September and the weather was temperate. I was feeling healthy and ambitious. The unemployment checks were still flowing in weekly, courtesy of last year's teaching gig. In the evenings, I'd get home from work, and my girlfriend (we'll call her Mary) would ask me, "How was your day?" And I'd respond, "Just fine." "What are you working on?" "Oh you know, this and that." It was all fine.

Is it worse to fail because you don't work hard enough, or to work hard and still fail anyway? I'm friends with a couple of pretty famous writers, have known them since before they got famous, and have seen it all change for them. They work hard. Harder than me? Hard to say. But they certainly are more famous.

How is everyone? Okay? Does anyone need to use the bathroom? If so, it's just down the hall, that way. The code for the men's is 534, and for the women, it's 512. I won't be getting to the heart of this for a while yet, so if you have to pee, or are just getting tired of hearing my voice, now would be a good time. I'll try not to take it personally.

September came and went, quickly. I'd come to know the space well by this point, had a good sense of the floor and of the building as a whole. And my work, such as it was, was getting ready to come along. I had been taking notes for the screenplay, a thriller set in Tajikistan about an American marine on three days' leave who saves a prostitute in trouble and as a result draws the ire of a shadowy international crime organization with links to the CIA and the Tajik government. The marine is forced to escape with the prostitute into Afghanistan through mountain passes used by heroin traffickers, refugees, and shepherds.

Of course, she's not really a prostitute, we discover . . . anyway you get the idea. I'd pitched it to my famous screenwriter friend, and he was quite positive about the whole thing, even offering to give it a read once I had a good draft, so that seemed promising. I'd been reading over the plays as well, was ready to plunge into rewrites of the tennis play, the camp play, and the Mexico play, all of which are very close. The residency was finally taking shape. I had tasks, and I had a plan.

And then came the stomachaches. And the cravings. I'd sit down at my desk by ten, spend an hour on the internet, and then, just as I was about to get to work, I'd find myself starving. And not just for any old thing: for doughnuts. And bagels. Starchy round things. As you may have noticed on your way here from the subway, there's a Dunkin' Donuts just up the block, about two hundred feet from here, on Maiden, just west of Pearl. You can see it from my office window. I should note that I have a complicated relationship with food, doughnuts in particular. I associate them with the darker periods of my existence, for example, in my mid-twenties when I'd start spontaneously crying in the Fine Fare on Avenue C, or after 9/11 when I put on fifteen pounds in a month. And of course my father loved his doughnuts. Very much.

So, doughnuts. First two, then three a day. I'd eat them in a single sitting, then check my Facebook page and wait for the sugar high. Once it hit, I'd start pacing through the office space, walking all the way to the far corners. Sometimes I'd even throw in a few pushups, or jumping jacks. The logic was that I was burning off the calories, evening myself out before getting back to work, but by the time I'd get back to my desk I'd be half comatose and the afternoon would be lost. I'd stick around for a few hours puttering about, then give up and head home. I must've seemed a little strange, or ill, because Mary started looking at me funny.

"Andy, are you okay?"

"Oh sure. I'm fine."

I was irritable, gaseous, and generally lethargic. I sensed the axe drawing closer, the day when the unemployment runs out, and the savings, and the office space, when Mary dumps me, and I lose the apartment, when I really do end up fat, middle-aged, unemployed, and entirely alone. Like my father.

But I soldiered on. And October approached November. The weather turned and the days darkened. On my famous screenwriter friend's advice, I'd shifted the setting of my screenplay from Tajikistan to Mauritania, and I was trying to come to terms with the full implications of that change. Sometimes I like to think with my head down on the desk, and as often as not my thinking turns to daydreaming turns into a full-fledged doze. I don't think it's necessarily a bad thing. After all, De Quincey was an opium addict, and Coleridge dreamed "Kubla Khan." Could I dream my thriller?

Here, come see my office.

Sorry, I know it's a pigsty. My dad's was worse. Picture this: Papers piled up on the desk, an ashtray overflowing (it was okay to smoke back then; everyone did it). Bookshelves with overstuffed binders teetering haphazardly, a spare pair of shoes, paperweights holding down sheaves of documents, chewing gum, candy wrappers and sandwich wrappers, mayonnaise-stained ties, his bosses used to come into his office and say, "Bragen, you're building a rat's nest in here," or, "Better get this office cleaned up, Bragen, before we take it and you to the garbage dump." Of course he always believed they were joking, my mother says, and he didn't change a thing. There was a dresser drawer back at home too, his drawer, full of broken watches, Camel unfiltered cigarette packs, spare keys, loose change, penny wrappers, paper clips, rubber bands, shoehorns, defunct bankbooks, and random business cards. I still remember its musty smell. I have a drawer like that too, in my old wooden desk at home, and if someday I have a son . . .

Don't worry. We're getting to the good part, I promise.

It was half dark when I woke up. I'd slipped down from my chair onto the carpet, was lying by the radiator. Wow, this carpet is soft, I thought. Why haven't I stretched out here before? Or have I? I felt like I had. I checked my phone. Three missed calls, all from Mary. And a text: "Where the hell are you?" We were supposed to meet for dinner. And go to the theater. The tickets were in my pocket. I'm usually very reliable, at least I used to be before I started this residency. Poor Mary. Even now, I can picture her waiting for me in the rain and the darkness.

So here I was, lying on the carpet in the dark, phone in hand, contemplating what I could possibly say to explain myself. And then I saw it. There in the radiator, just sticking out of the grate. For a minute it looked like a crayon melting. I reached toward the grate, grabbed it by the edge, and pulled it out.

[*He produces a photo.*]

That's right. It's a Polaroid. How did I miss it? I thought I'd explored this office pretty carefully after all. I examined it under the glow of my cell phone.

As soon as I saw the image I jumped up, though I didn't understand why. It was just an office photo, right? Maybe even from here. The carpeting looked similar. I gave it a closer look. There was a Christmas tree in the background. Fully decorated. And what looked like a punch bowl. An office Christmas party. Three friends around a punch bowl raising glasses. Two men in shirtsleeves with loud ties, one skinny and mustachioed, the other broad-shouldered with a full head of silvery gray hair, and between them a woman with a Santa hat in her hand. She was tall and thin, with long legs and high heels, with curly brown hair that . . . Holy shit. Is that . . . Nancy? My dad's secretary? In here? Could it be . . . ?

Now that I had an inkling about where I was, I started running all around the whole floor. I zoomed back and forth from corner to corner and soon enough my feet found their way to the original layout. Obviously, everything here has been replaced and renovated several times to the point where it's barely recognizable. But amazingly much of the structure is the same. Out here you had your office cubicles for various functionaries and a row of windowed offices for those who were slightly higher up. The executives tended to cluster on the east side of the building where the views are better. And of course there was the stockroom, which we'll get to in a moment.

I was a huge baseball fan as a kid. Harold (my dad) grew up just outside of Boston, had been a fan of the Boston Braves and to a lesser extent the Red Sox. He'd given it up as an adult, but now that he had a son he got back into it, throwing his support behind the Yankees. We'd go to several games a year, generally on weeknights. Usually my dad would be working before the game so I'd go down to his office to meet him. I'd check in at the front desk and Nancy would come get me. She was in her thirties at the time, I'm guessing, and boy did she love me. When she saw me she'd put on such a smile. "Come on, Andy, how about a 7UP?" I was like, "Yes, please." And she would serve me 7UP in a glass. "I bet I know what you want to do." "Uh-huh." And she would take me to my favorite place. Come on, I'll show you.

As much as I love offices, I love office stockrooms even more. There are so many great things in here. Boxes of pens, notepads, binders, glue sticks, tape, paper clips, Liquid Paper, Post-it Notes. Typing paper, reams of it, and copy paper too. Boxes of pencils with erasers, binder clips, and my favorite, rubber bands. Even now, in this nearly empty space, I can picture the metal shelving, I can smell the toner.

She had amazing legs, my dad had told me, legs up to here, and so, ever the obedient child, I looked at them. I didn't see what the big deal was—they just looked like legs, skinnier than my mom's for sure, but generally similar, though I'd never actually seen my mom in stockings. Or high heels. Everything about her was at a funny angle cause of the heels. They were gigantic. She'd kick them off before climbing up the ladder to get down the Presto Magix. (I'll get to those in a bit.) One time she caught me looking up her skirt . . . she had this black underwear on that I know now is pretty fancy. Some years later, when Leslie Nielsen and Priscilla Presley had their infamous exchange in *Naked Gun* ("Nice beaver," "Thank you, I just had it stuffed"), I thought of her immediately.

November came and went and with it, Thanksgiving. Mary joined some of her graduate school friends for a meal, but I bowed out. I was battling an awful cold at the time, a valid excuse because who wants to infect anyone, but I wasn't entirely unhappy. Not that I didn't like her friends, a charming, handsome, and energetic set, mostly in their mid-twenties, but I did at times feel like the creepy old man in the cardigan.

Meanwhile, the screenplay was proceeding apace. I had been reading about Mauritania (did you know there's still slavery there), and had come to realize that perhaps it wasn't the best location for a feature film. Turkey seemed like a better idea. Or perhaps Bulgaria. They say the Balkans are a hive of intrigue.

How many of you recall Presto Magix? You have your sheet of paper with a blank yet evocative landscape—a pirate ship on the high seas or dark and venomous Gotham, Superman's small town or Spidey's city, and you have a sheet of rub-off characters and objects—heroes and villains, weapons, you name it. You rub the character sheet with a pencil, like so, and the characters stick to the landscape wherever you put them. Within the, I grant you, somewhat limited parameters, you make up your own story, your own comic strip. Fun stuff, right? We used to get them out of the stockroom. There were thousands of them there. Of all different types. Presto Magix was a client, that's why. Of

Market Facts. My dad's old company. He worked there for years, from the mid-seventies into the early eighties. There or rather here, because his office was here. That's right, here, in this very office space. In this very office, the one with my name on it. What an amazing coincidence, huh? Almost too weird to be true. For some reason, I'd had it in my head that the company was located in midtown, on Madison, around Fiftieth, near the Bagel Nosh that used to be there, but clearly I'd been mistaken. This was it: my dad worked here. It's no wonder I jumped up. You would too if faced with that sort of déjà vu.

Everyone okay out there? Matters are not proceeding as fast as I'd hoped they would, and for that I'm sorry. I will get to the point, very soon, I promise.

Market Facts was a well-established market research firm, one of the big boys. Market research is an offshoot of advertising, a study of how best to promote products. This was a second career for him. After Yale, where he was awarded the Whitbread Prize for literature, my dad went to Berkeley to get a PhD in English. He got through the master's degree and then stalled. He spent several years teaching at various universities but never finished the PhD. After he'd gotten married and had a child (me), my mother gave him an ultimatum: either you finish your dissertation or you get a job. In 1976, he joined Market Facts. He was thirty-eight at the time. I'm thirty-nine.

One time my dad and I went over to Nancy's apartment. I'm not sure just when it was, though I'm thinking that it might have been over a weekend. I remember Dad was in jeans, and loafers. I think she was in sweatpants though I could be wrong. This I do know: she wasn't wearing heels. She turned on the stereo, then poured my dad a drink (probably J&B on the rocks, that was his favorite), and had one herself. She opened up a warm eight-ounce bottle of 7UP for me and filled what must have been a highball glass with ice. I was installed on a stool at the kitchen bar with a couple of Presto Magix sheets (The Fantastic

Four? Underdog?), and my dad and she retreated to the living room for what was, I guess, a private conversation.

I am picturing her place as a kind of seventies bachelorette pad. A one bedroom, long and thin, with the kitchenette up front near the entrance, with steps down to the living room, with its black leather couch and glass coffee table—everything dark and cool. The bedroom is beyond.

You see this scar, here on the first joint of my thumb? I've always been a klutz. As I was finishing with my second Presto Magix (Mr. Magoo? Super Friends?), rubbing off one last character, my hand slipped and there the 7UP bottle went, right off the table. It was glass, of course, back then plastic bottles were just catching on, and as I saw it falling, I jumped off the stool and reached for it, and I got a shard right in here. Before I knew it, Nancy was there, holding me. There was a lot of blood, and it got all over her blouse. She wrapped my thumb in a cloth and held it to stem the bleeding. Then she disinfected it with Merthiolate and wrapped it with gauze and Band-Aids. My dad stood beside her and looked on admiringly at her skills. As for me, the experience was sensual, almost sexual.

My body doesn't always do what I want it to do, which is a kind of failure. I slip, or I stumble or I bump into walls, I double-fault on my tennis serve, or run out of gas after just a mile or two on the track. The coughs, the sneezes, the farts, those gray hairs popping up everywhere. The sore knees, the stiff jaw, the headaches and stomachaches, the lost hard-ons, the hard-ons that don't come at all. This body that fails, that lets me down, that lets other people down. (Sorry, Mary.)

December was cold and icy. I'd been the picture of health over the summer, but like the weather, I had deteriorated. Stairs winded me, and my belly, once reasonably flat, was puckering out. Over the summer Mary had talked about taking me home to meet the family, but I guess she'd thought better of it because no invite was forthcoming. I understood. She'd had a hard autumn, and probably needed a break, from New York, and work, and me. So there I was, home alone. It was not where I wanted to be, especially during the holidays. So I did the sensible thing: I grabbed my sleeping bag and came down here.

Hi, Melissa. Hi, Sean. I know you guys said at our Lower Manhattan Cultural Council orientation that if we slept down here you'd expel us from the residency. Let me just say that this is all in the past, that those days are past and I sleep here rarely if ever, so please, please don't fire me.

It was a whole new experience, the office at night. Once all the other artists had gone home, I'd stealthily unfurl my sleeping bag and curl up next to the radiator. I had a good supply of ramen, so the hot pot was great for food. I put up the blinds in the executive bathroom just in case there were any security guards in the building across the way. I'd wash up in there, giving myself a sponge bath, and settle into my office with a murder mystery and a hot toddy. Or I'd hold a movie night, combining both work and play by watching thrillers on my computer. The screenplay had made what I hoped was its final move, to Berlin, always a great setting for international intrigue. I wasn't sure exactly what mountains our hero would be escaping over (The Alps? The Carpathians?), but I was sure I'd come up with something. I'd taken to buying boxes of doughnuts from the grocery store, some chocolate glazed, some pure chocolate on chocolate. I'd eat four at a time, and then make my way to the toilet down the hall. The sickness in my stomach, the dry mouth, the low-grade diarrhea, it brought me back to my twenties, those years alone in that old rundown apartment on Avenue C, the daily rice and beans lunches at Casa Adela, the Chinese takeout, that girl, what was her name, with the dyed blond hair, who worked as a PA, she had those industrial blinds that let no light in so you never knew if it was day or night. Or Olga the Russian, who was in the roller-blading accident—we broke up not long before Christmas, wow, that was a hard holiday. (Jesus, have all of my relationships ended right before the holidays? Have I spent every December alone?)

I got it in my head to track down Nancy. I'd been wondering what had happened to her. Was she still at Market Facts? It seemed unlikely, since I couldn't even find the company on the web. Besides, by now she was probably in her late sixties and retired. And of course, I didn't even know her last name.

It took me a day. Between Facebook and Google, there really is no place to hide anymore. She had indeed retired, and had moved to Florida with her husband, another former Market Facts employee.

I went ahead and taped the call. I thought it would be good to have some kind of record of my investigation.

[*He plays a tape recording of the conversation.*]

Hello.

Hello. Is this Nancy?

Who is calling?

This is Andy Bragen.

Andy who?

I'm Harold's son.

Harold?

Harold Bragen. He worked with you.

Harold Bragen. Harold Bragen. Oh . . . Harold Bragen.

. . .

Bill, it's Harold Bragen on the phone!

No, no, it's not. I'm his son. Andy.

Who?

His son.

Andrew?

That's right.

Andrew. You were so small.

. . .

I was wrong. It's Andrew. His son.

HIS SON!

You must be all grown by now. How old are you? Twenty-five?

Thirty-nine, actually.

My oh my.

I'm just wondering about Market Facts. The office was downtown, right?

I haven't been to New York in years. The city's changed, I hear.

It was on Maiden Lane, right? Between Water and Pearl?

You were a strange little child. So solitary. Always playing by yourself, scratching away at those funny little games we had.

Presto Magix.

Who's that?

Presto Magix. That was the name of the game.

Oh boy, those were some neat times. Me, Harold, and Frank, we had some neat times.

Frank who?

The whole profession has changed now, that's what Bill says. The quality of data has just dropped through the floor.

My dad said the same thing.

How is Harold these days?

Harold died.

No, he didn't.

I'm afraid so.

No no no no. He was far too young for that.

He was seventy-one.

My Bill, he's eighty-two, and strong as an ox. What did Harold die of?

Liver cancer.

Oh God. That's the worst. Andrew, I'm so sorry.

It's okay.

No really. You poor thing.

It's been a couple of years actually.

Trust me, that kind of pain never goes away.

Listen, I had a question for you. You may remember, my dad got fired. I was just wondering if you had any idea why?

Why would I know why?

Did you two ever . . . I mean, there was that time at your apartment, when I cut my thumb, and you bandaged me. And then you had those high heels. Did you two ever . . .

Me and your dad? Are you kidding me?

I thought maybe . . .

BILL, WHY DID YOU FIRE HAROLD?

. . .

HAROLD!

He's getting a little deaf.

Bill and I, we met there. At Market Facts. Our first kiss, it was in the stockroom. He was married at the time, a silver-haired stallion. A little heavy, yes, but I took care of that soon enough.

Okay, okay! I'm getting to it!

Young man, it's been a pleasure talking to you. Please give my best to Harold.

Like I said, he's . . .

[*Dial tone.*]

I understood my mistake then. I'd only had eyes for Nancy, and so I'd overlooked all of the other evidence in the Polaroid. The broad-shouldered man, with the silvery gray hair: that was Bill, the silver-haired stallion. And then, there on the left, that must be . . . Frank. Of course. Frank McGrew. Suddenly it all came back to me.

Everyone okay, bladder-wise? I do go on, I know. My father went on. I have to admit that over those last several years sometimes he would get to talking and I would tune him out, checking my email or flipping through TV channels. There is always that question: If I'd listened more closely, if I'd given more thought to my father's experience of the world, would I have noticed when he first started getting sick?

For example, when he visited me in Minneapolis, six months before he died. I was out there on a fellowship at the time, subletting a small professor's house just off of Lake Street (the house being small, not the professor). Harold came out for the weekend. It was the longest consecutive time I'd spent with him in years. We went to a theater performance and a Twins game. We ate a couple of good meals and went out for beers. Once, I ran ahead to catch a bus and he chased after me and stumbled and nearly fell. And then, after we'd walked from Uptown along a couple of lakes to the Walker, a distance of about a mile, he got pretty winded. And, he'd lost a bunch of weight, without even trying, which he was happy about. And he had a persistent, if intermittent, cough. Beyond all that, there was something in his face. Suddenly he looked old.

My mother is full of theories as to why he died. There was a fall he took in a parking garage, about four months before the diagnosis. He never checked it out, and her notion was that he'd broken a rib, and that the friction might have infected the liver. And of course there was his drinking. He wasn't an alcoholic, but some people are more susceptible than others. Or his eating habits. According to my mother, before they got married, he spent a whole year in Indiana teaching English and eating nothing but Arby's roast beef sandwiches. By the end of their marriage, he weighed over 240. He always did love his fast food. And his doughnuts. Very much.

Let's move on, shall we? I want to show you the conference room. It's just down this way. Here on the right is what used to be a small audiovisual room. Here on the left, by the windows, is where the main reception was: two secretaries behind a rounded black Formica desk. As you can see, we've got a good view of the building across the street. All those other offices. All those other lives. Often I'll lunch out here just to watch them busily working away. Then again, since I can see them, they can also see me through my office window, napping, putting my feet up on the desk, eating my ramen, or my doughnuts.

Of course, in late December most of the offices across the way were empty. I'm speaking of Christmas Eve, which, as you may recall, fell on a Thursday. As a child, I sang in the boys choir at Grace Church, on Broadway and Tenth. It was a job, I should mention. They paid us a small hourly stipend. Grace Church is Episcopal, and on the traditional side, and we choirboys would wear white robes with ribbon necklaces indicating our rank (I rose as far as Lead Chorister, second in command!). On Christmas Eve, we'd lead the processional, carrying candles and singing "O Come, All Ye Faithful." We'd enter the church through a large oak door adjacent to a small chapel and take a left toward the entrance, where we'd turn and head up the main aisle to the altar, where our pews were.

So, here I was, on the night before Christmas, all on my own. It was on the cold side—I guess the management figured that, since the building was empty, they might as well turn the heat down. Bundled up in pajamas, a sweater, and an old red bathrobe that I'd inherited from my dad, I engaged in my own processional. "O come, all ye faithful, joyful and triumphant, O come ye, O come ye, to Bethlehem." No eyes upon me, no candle, I walked down the hall, over there to the east side, over by the executive office, then back this way right over here, right into the belly of the beast.

This is the conference room. Pretty nice, right? Back then, this room had a long table. It was a kind of boardroom and sometimes doubled as an executive lunchroom. Frank, of course, wasn't an executive, he was a step down from my father, who had just moved up to his own windowed office, so I gather that he couldn't even have been in here that day if not for my dad.

One day near the end, when he was particularly lucid, he said to me, "I wake up in the mornings and I want to weep." "Do you weep?" I asked. "Yes, I do." There he was, in his bedroom, his death room, Cynthia, the Ghanaian hospice aide, cleaning him, collecting his shit and pee, trying to coax him into drinking one more Ensure, just to get his strength up. For those three weeks, his last on earth, she was someone I could trust. She felt like part of the family. I haven't spoken to her since.

Where was I? That's right: back to Frank. He's the skinny guy in the photo, the one with the mustache. Looking at him now I start to wonder if he wasn't some kind of cokehead. He used to go to Yankee games with my dad and me. They talked work and baseball while I watched the action and ate Cracker Jacks by the handful.

A couple of times he lit up a joint. I knew what a joint was even back then, knew that smell from the playground by my house. I don't know why my dad never smoked with Frank. Maybe he was worried I would tell on him. I did in fact tell on Frank, mentioning it to my mom when we were out getting ice cream one day, and I don't think he came to any more ballgames with us after that, though the cause could well have been something else, as you'll see.

I don't know what they were arguing about in here, but it did seem pretty heated. Harold had his back to us. He was standing, leaning on the long table toward Frank, who was still seated. My dad's chair had fallen over backward. His combed-over hair, normally held in place with Vitalis, was practically standing on end, mad-professor style.

"How could you do this to me?"

"Take it easy, Hal."

"You son-of-a-bitch!"

And he slammed his fist into the table, sending his half-full coffee mug clattering onto the carpet.

"Harold," Nancy said.

And he turned around. He had this wild look in his eyes. He held her glance for a second, then stomped past us, out of the conference room, off to the men's room I guess, or maybe his office.

Nancy brought me to her desk. She sat me down with a Presto Magix (Animals of Africa, my favorite) and rushed off. No 7UP, no nothing. Within twenty minutes or so, my father showed up. He'd changed into jeans. We left immediately for the ballgame, just the two of us. Frank's seat remained empty, and my father, while he did buy me peanuts and a hot dog, seemed tense, and distracted. We left the game early, after the seventh inning, which was the first time we'd ever done that.

And then he got fired. One day in the spring of 1982, Market Facts let him go. He was forty-four at the time, just five years older than I am now.

He would live another two-and-a-half decades, but I keep coming back to this moment. Here a path started, a pattern that stayed with him for the rest of his life. Some lowlights include a new job for a smaller firm that lasted three months, another year out of work, meetings of the forty-plus club, a gathering of unemployed executives at least as desperate as he. And my mother, imploring him to pull himself together: "Get a job somewhere," she said. "I'm working on it." "Get a job somewhere, anywhere: as a waiter, as a salesman, at Saks or Macy's or McDonalds—wherever you can." The loveless marriage that lingered on, more doughnuts, more pounds, weekday afternoons napping in the easy chair, Dad you want to play catch, sorry I'm tired, he was always so tired, his unemployment a secret at school, none of my friends, none of my friends' parents could know. How about doorman, that's a job? His shame, this secret shame that he bore, this impotence. He bore it, we all bore it, I bore it with him, for years.

I picture him getting fired. Bill would have called him into the corner office and passed on the word. Or maybe it wasn't Bill, maybe it was a lower-level person who fired him, right here in the conference room. They'd be apologetic yet firm, and my father, still prideful, would say in a small voice, okay, fine, thank you, I'll just finish up what I've been doing and . . . no need, they say. It's all taken care of. And he'd go back to his office with an empty box from the stockroom and start packing up his belongings. The spare pair of shoes, the extra belt, the mayonnaise-stained ties. The scientific calculator. The stapler. The paperweight. He had a plastic photo cube, with two photos of me, one from when I was five, half toothless in my Mickey Mouse shirt, another taken at the ballpark from just that past year.

I do like to light up periodically myself. It's not a habit I'm proud of, nor one that I actually can afford given my current financial state. But certainly, over the years, I've done my share of inhaling. I'd thought of getting some for my father when he was dying, but he ended up not needing it. One of the upsides of liver failure is that the ammonia that gets released by the failing organ acts as a natural painkiller. The downside of that upside is that the patient's brain gets cloudy, and lucidity and focus slip quickly away. Within a month of our visit to the oncologist in late September, my father as I had known him was only intermittently present. All in the space of a few days he lost interest in music, words, television, almost everything. I would read the columnists to him, Krugman and Brooks, and they would occasionally pique his interest, but for the most part he couldn't focus.

So, Christmas Eve, in the conference room. I have a half-eaten box of chocolate doughnuts and a half-drunk fifth of J&B Scotch. I've got a bowl from St. Mark's Place, and a dime bag from Washington Square Park. It's gotten even colder in here and I'm wearing my winter coat over the bathrobe and pj's, have wrapped a blanket around my knees.

I ate, I drank, I toked up, and I remembered. Remembered walking down that aisle as a choirboy. Remembered Christmas Eves and New Year's Eves in my twenties spent alone with Henry James and Sam Cooke, and a sadness, an immense misery, which I reveled in, drinking myself into a self-pitying stupor.

And now, 2013—the year I turn forty. Mid-life, by most standards. Worse, in my case, since my father and grandfather both died in their early seventies. A decade for gray hairs, belly fat, and divorce. A decade when you no longer buy the lies you've been telling yourself. Maybe it's harder for women, with menopause and all, with hot flashes, but when things fall apart for men, I feel like it goes deeper. I've seen it a few times. With Harold of course. With my uncle who lost a child. With Mary's dad, who's had his challenges. Something cracks, and these men, they are never the same. I'm so scared of that, of being broken by this life, of something happening, something small perhaps but significant, an event from which I will never recover.

We think we're escaping it, that we've found a way to avoid the legacy, but of course we walk right into it. I've always worked for myself, which means no one can fire me, but isn't failing the same as getting fired? For example, if I want to have a kid, I'll probably have to change careers, and the nearly twenty years I've put into playwriting and theater will be lost. I'll be starting at the bottom rung with the twenty-five-year-olds, and when the next recession hits, I'll be the first one they let go. Like my dad.

The booze was gone. The doughnuts too. What else could I do but light up again? It had been a while since I'd last smoked, and the effect was . . . surprising. They say marijuana is stronger than it used to be and I believe it. It was all quite delightful. Finally, I had clarity. This is my life. All alone on Christmas Eve, wrapped in a down coat and a sleeping bag, with a hat on, haven't shaved in four days, nails chewed to the bone, haven't done a lick of work in weeks (let's be honest here), homeless in an office that's no longer an office in a conference room that hasn't hosted a conference in years, slowly sinking into a mire of my own making, into my own deep and full, rich and loamy self-pitying patheticness, what could make this even more pathetic (I thought as I puffed away), what could make it even sadder (as I checked my Facebook page), even more disgusting (as I farted, as I belched, as I licked up the crumbs), wallow Andy wallow cause this is it, the bottom, the gloriously delightful hopelessly happy stoned-out-of-my-gourd BOTTOM.

And then, the fire alarm.

Oh shit. Now I've done it.

Beep beep beep. They're going to come up. They're going to find me and arrest me and throw me out and send me home and I can't go home I can't be alone in that apartment, too many years too many relationships blown apart, and now with Mary away for the holidays have I blown it with her too? Beep beep beep. Jesus, I've got to do something.

[*He starts waving the smoke away.*]

That's it. Dissipate. Dissipate. Beep beep beep. And what if they find my belongings? It's clear isn't it that someone's living here, that's it I'll shove it all into the closet, the doughnut boxes, the pillow, the blankets, beep beep beep the journal, the books, the DVDs, the soda cans, the fast-food wrappers, beep beep beep, the hat, the gloves, me. Me! I stuffed me in the closet. I hid in the back corner, curling up like a child who knows he's about to get punished. I closed my eyes and awaited my fate.

Time passed. Nothing. The alarm bell had stopped. I checked the time on my watch. Ten minutes to midnight. Wow. Nearly Christmas. I watched the second hand twirl down toward the six, and then back around, seven, eight, nine, ten, eleven, twelve . . .

And then I heard it. The whirring of an elevator engine. It was rising, rising, toward my floor. Slowing down. Stopping. Opening. Clomp clomp clomp. Clomp clomp clomp: the firemen, with their equipment. Clomp. Clomp. Clomp. They're looking around the floor. Don't come in here please. Whatever you do, don't look in here. Clomp. My eyes are shut so tight. I hear the door opening, that door there, the conference room door, they're poking around, somehow they know it was set off in here. Please don't fire me. Please, I'm begging you. If I lose this, I'll lose everything. How could I face myself? How could I admit this to anyone? Oh God, I'm so ashamed. Clomp clomp clomp. They're looking around the room. They're opening the closets, drawing closer drawing closer step by step by step until they're here they're opening the door on me they . . . they . . .

Hi, Dad.

There he was. My dad. Looking young, like the Harold of my earliest memories. There he was, right in front of me, my father vintage 1977. Before the firings, the divorce, the cancer, the death. He's thirty-nine years old, he is five foot ten, 185, not exactly Adonis, but it could be worse. He even has a little hair left. He looks down at me. I don't know what he sees there, the thirty-nine-year-old or the child, but whatever it is, he isn't too impressed.

What are you doing down there, squirt?

Nothing.

Come on. We'll throw the ball around.

You want to throw the ball around?

Sure. We'll head out to the playground.

It's freezing out.

It's never too cold for a game of catch.

Why are you here, Dad?

I took a day off.

Did they fire you?

Are you kidding? Me? Never.

Dad, I'm in trouble.

You seem like you're all right.

I'm not.

How about some Orchidia?

They closed. In the eighties.

We'll have the Orchidia Special and a beer.

A beer?

Sure. Why not? I'll go call ahead.

Dad? Dad?

But he was gone.

And I was lying here, curled up in the corner, freezing. Somehow I'd fallen asleep. I'd shat myself, just like him.

Everyone okay? Never fear, we're almost there. It's time to move on to brighter pastures, to see how the other half works. That's right, we're visiting the executive office. My father never made it to this level. He got beyond the cubicle stage, made it as far as vice president at one or two small companies, though actually that wasn't anything special, as most of these companies had several vice presidents. No, let me take that back. He did make it. I found this card the other day, a whole box-ful, actually. Here you go.

[*He passes out the cards.*]

Harold Bragen—President, Nomad Travel Bazaar—New Jersey, Inc., Nomad Travel, the only job he never got fired from. That's because I was his boss. Nomad had once been mine. I'd worked for a couple of other travel companies, under the table mostly, and had decided to branch out on my own, to open a small home-based agency. This was back in the nineties when the internet was just starting to catch on. I was not long out of college, was trying to figure out how to make a living and be a writer. Nomad turned out to be a pretty good solution: I was working less than full-time and yet I was making good money.

The problem was that I was ashamed of it. I'd go to parties with certain friends and they'd introduce me as a travel agent. Inevitably a question about deals would follow. Or sometimes I would mumble something about being a playwright, and they'd ask me if I'd had anything done that they would have heard of and of course the answer was no.

Harold took over Nomad in 2001. He knew I was thinking of shutting it down to focus on my writing and so he offered to run it for me. Technically I was his boss, but truth is he worked for himself, for the first time in his life. It was a real third act for him, and he put everything he had into it. Unlike me, this was what he wanted to be doing. He seemed . . . happy. Our conversations got more frequent, and whereas in the past they'd revolved around baseball or politics, now we focused on airline tickets. It was intimacy, of a sort. I would collect money from the business just about every month, and he would lie to me and tell me he was paying himself just as much. I never looked too carefully at the accounting, maybe because inside I knew that he was working for just about nothing, that he was in it purely for the pleasure of helping, for the pride and dignity he got from running his own business.

Harold worked from home. His office, such as it was, was in his living room, stuffed in a corner, over by a window. Picture this: two folding tables supporting two desktop computers with grimy keyboards covered with coffee stains and English muffin crumbs. Piles of paper strewn about across the tables and thrown into various boxes, a system that only he could understand. His hutch, from my grandmother, full of mailing labels, old receipts, and pricing binders. The printer, which I now have in my own home office. And a third computer, a Toshiba laptop he'd bought just two months before the diagnosis, which I will inherit, which I will write this play on.

He lived alone in Secaucus, New Jersey, in Harmon Cove Towers. Google it sometime and you'll get a good look at the place. It's a high-rise apartment complex just minutes from the city, two big buildings in the middle of what once was swampland. Inside, the building's hallways are carpeted and the concierges are at their desks 24/7. My father was comfortable there, though to me it always felt depressing, and isolating. It was close, but I didn't get out there very often, at least not until Harold got sick.

That June, before the diagnosis, he was making uncharacteristic mistakes. He'd always tended to procrastinate, but now it was worse than ever. When I'd ask him about it, he was full of excuses as to why he hadn't sent in for a refund for X person, or why he hadn't FedExed the ticket to Y person. I remember getting short with him on the phone. My thought at the time was, well, yeah, I'd have fired him too. What a disaster this guy is. He can't even run this little tiny business. Harold Bragen: a total fucking failure. But I was wrong. He was sick. He was dying. And he'd done so much so well.

There's one more place we have to go: Harold's bedroom. That's right. This way. Come on in. He put up the wallpaper himself. You see that worn spot? That was where he used to rest the pillow while reading in bed. To the left was the humidifier, which ran throughout his sickness, a constant low hum. Across from the bed was a bookshelf, full of texts, read and unread. The Lyndon Johnson biographies by Caro and Dallek (all of them read). Nabokov's *Ada*. Niall Ferguson's *The War of the World*, a gift from me, *A Complete History of the Negro Leagues*, a gift from me, *Innumeracy*, all about math, some puzzle books, some Melville, etc., etc. (He kept his Henry James collection, which I now have, in the spare bedroom.) Next to the shelf was a small metal stand for the TV and DVD player, along with his DVD library: *The Sopranos* season five, *Angels in America*, *The Constant Gardener*, *Talk to Her*, *The Sopranos* season four, the thriller written by my famous friend, *Sense and Sensibility*, *Gangs of New York*, *The Aviator*. It was kind of a random collection—I can't decide whether he'd joined a movie club or just grabbed whatever seemed interesting when at the bookstore. The room was dark; the shades were drawn. Over there, where you're standing, he had an ottoman in front of an easy chair. I'd tried to pull him up onto it one night in late October, when I'd been woken up by moaning sounds. He'd fallen on his way back from the bathroom and was on the floor shivering, naked but for a pair of soiled underwear. When I couldn't get him up (he'd lost weight but was still big), I called the police, and they came by and helped him back into bed. This had happened before, I later learned. He'd woken up on the bathroom floor, covered in shit, unable to move. No one was there with him, so he just lay there until the Ambien wore off. I didn't know how bad it was at the time. I'd call him every day to check in, and once he alluded elliptically to a little incident, a slight annoyance that he'd taken care of, only telling me days later, once I'd realized that he couldn't be left alone anymore.

This is where he will die. On Monday, November 19, just before noon, I will receive a call from Cynthia, the home health aide, and I will jump in a taxi to Penn Station, then a train to Secaucus Junction, and then a taxi to his apartment. He is in his bed, moaning. His extremities are frigid, and his eyes keep rolling up into his head. I hold his hand some, not that he is aware of it, and check email on my phone. I've been managing Nomad during his sickness, am dealing with a demanding client, an eighty-year-old Italian woman who's pestering me for fax itineraries. So I'm running in and out of the room to deal with that. Meanwhile, all I can do is wait.

He died at five, and shortly thereafter we ordered a pizza. Mary was here, she'd arrived around four, as was Cynthia. I started letting people know, via email mostly, though I did call my mother, and my father's brother. We all knew it was coming, so our sadness was muted. When the pizza arrived, Mary, Cynthia, and I sat down at the table for a quiet dinner. I drank a glass of Scotch, raising it in honor of my father. In the morning the undertaker came and carried him off. And the home health service sent a car for Cynthia and she left. Mary left too, as she had to work that day. I dealt with some Nomad business and started looking through his papers, sorting through files. I didn't know what else to do. Later, before I left his apartment, I read Yeats's "Sailing to Byzantium" out loud and drank another glass of Scotch.

It wasn't until a few days later, when I was cleaning out his hutch, that I found his poems. They were typed on a manual typewriter in the early to mid-sixties, when he was a graduate student at Berkeley. They're terrible. My father, for all his wonderful qualities, was not a poet. And yet I read them very carefully, looking for clues about him, just as I would look at his photos and try to figure out who he was and what was going on with him aside from weight fluctuation. Many of them were about the Cold War, which given their vintage I guess makes sense.

I had thought to finish by reading you one of them. In fact, when I was writing this piece in my office, I thought, tonight when I go home, I'll dig up that old folder full of typewritten poems on yellowing paper out of my filing cabinet. Which I did. I read them all over again, for the first time in over a year. As I said, they were terrible, but that wasn't the issue. The issue was that he didn't seem to be in them. Or if he was, I couldn't figure out where. I looked everywhere in them for a clue, but like with the Polaroid, he wasn't there.

And so . . . Back to Christmas Day. To Christmas morning. I wake up in my office with a bit of a hangover, with the foggy brain that I get from smoking too much grass. It's a sunny morning, bright light glowing through the windows. Part of me feels like Ebenezer Scrooge, joyous because I've seen a ghost, but the night is over and I'm here to tell the tale. Part of me feels very alone. I'd like to tell you that I picked up the phone and called Mary. That I reached out to her and everything was okay. I'd like to tell you that, but it's not quite true. I didn't call her just then because I still needed to be alone, I still had more to remember. And I did just that. I sat down at my desk that morning, and I remembered, a long list of things about my father:

his black socks

his Camels

his handkerchiefs (I use them now)

the pizza we ate together (at the Orchidia and elsewhere)

his glasses (quite thick)

his comb-over

his hat

his voice

his handwriting (worse than mine)

those gyros we ate in Astoria

that trip we took together just the two of us, to look at colleges

the meal we had together, me, him, and Mary, as he was dying (The Bonefish Grill. Yuck.)

his puzzles

his books

his mind

his ears (they grew)

his teeth (false, I threw them away)

his nose

his lips (dry toward the end)

his eyes (tired)

his love.

Oh God. His love.

I'm gonna let you go soon. Let me just add that I'm super glad you're here. It's nice of you to come to hear this story, considering how many other things you must have to do. We're all so busy, right? Rest assured, you will be rewarded. We have doughnuts and wine waiting, a little reception in Harold's honor, a chance to chat and raise a glass. No obligation, or expectations, but we'd love to meet you.

One last thing. One last memory. That of my father, remembering his father. He told me this story on our drive back to Secaucus from the oncologist, right after he'd been given the death sentence. It was 1974, the summer of my first birthday. His father, David Bragen, in his late sixties at the time, came to Britain to visit my parents, who'd rented a cottage there for August. David had had a couple of strokes, and was nearly blind. He wanted to hold me, and he held me in his arms. So here we are, my dad and I, driving on the turnpike. I joked, "It's a wonder he didn't drop me." My father didn't hesitate: "He would never drop you," he said. "He would never let that happen." Thank you.

Notes on My Mother's Decline

Notes on My Mother's Decline was originally produced for the stage in New York City by The Play Company (Kate Loewald, Founding Producer; Robert G. Bradshaw, Managing Director) and Andy Bragen Theatre Projects in October 2019 at Next Door at New York Theatre Workshop. The cast was as follows:

Mother . . . . Caroline Lagerfelt

Son . . . . Ari Fliakos

The production was directed by Knud Adams, the set design was by Marsha Ginsberg, the costume design was by Sophia Choi, the lighting design was by Oona Curley, the sound design was by Peter Mills Weiss, the projection design was by Knud Adams, and the stage manager was Molly Shea.

CHARACTERS

Mother speaks the lines in bold
Son speaks the lines that aren't in bold

Winter—late 2013. Three months before my daughter was born.

A beginning, or rather a place to begin.

It is late morning.
She is in her bed.
(That giant bed, covered with pillows and towels and old mail, with her handbag, and her cane.)
She naps, a book on her chest.
A TV across from her, the Weather Channel on, muted.
She naps.
She wakes.
She lights a cigarette, and smokes.
She picks up the receiver on her phone and listens. No messages.
She opens a Mason jar full of coffee and drinks from it.
She reads.
She smokes.
She naps.
A visitor. (me)

She is startled.
Gasp.

You startled me.

Let me count it.

I'll write you a check.

The stupidifier needs to be filled.

Thank you. Do you have them facing the right way?

The big black arrows. They need to be facing forward.

No. Not really. I'm not okay.

Well no, just down.

Bradley's sick and in the hospital, and Robert Heidel died.

One of the dentists.

I'm writing his wife in Mexico.

**He was a real macho man. A man's man. They lost a child in 9/11.
I cannot imagine.**

Call me to check in.

Okay bye.

She smokes.
She naps.

A visitor. (me)
She is startled.

I do keep track of it.

I do!

I went through my checkbook. I made a list. Every time I had you bring me money. See here? See? Two thousand here. Two thousand here. Michelle gets groceries. And Vince. And Rose. It's Christmastime. It is important to tip people who work for you at Christmastime. That is what proper people do.

I am a rich woman.

I am a frugal woman.

No need. It's all fine. I am a happy camper.

Did I have any mail?

You didn't check, did you?

A person could check the mail sometimes. When they're coming up. Or check for packages. When they're passing by, on their way home from the subway. You do come past here, right?

Two minutes of your time. Just pop in the lobby, see if there are packages.

Fine. Do what you can. Thank you.

How about a hug?

Love you, sweet angel.

Make sure to slam the door shut on the way out so it locks.

She smokes.

She reads.

Pee-time—she hobbles to the bathroom.

Onto the toilet—she pees.

The phone rings.

Hobblehobble—back to the bedroom.

She misses the call.

She is out of breath.

She falls back onto the bed, and swings her legs up, getting back into position.

She picks up the phone and checks the message.

She coughs and more pee leaks out.

She places a call. To Bob.

Bob? You there?

She smokes.

She checks her appointment book.

The phone rings.

Bob.

I was in the kitchen.

We know we can't believe the reviews.

Who cares about the *Times*?

The *Journal* loved it.

Terry Teachout said it was ten best of the year.

What else? Any hot news?

Oh yes. Mr. Hare. My favorite.

No. I can't.

You know I don't do Broadway. All those stairs.

And the crowds. The traffic. Marco has nowhere to bring around the car.

Bob-I-don't-do-Broadway-anymore-and-that's-final.

She smokes.

She naps.

She drinks cold coffee from a Mason jar.

She drinks seltzer from a bottle.

The Weather Channel is on, muted.

She eats blackberries.

She drinks coffee.

She smokes.

(This is a home that smells like smoke. It smells of smoke so deep that you are aware of it in the building's hallways, when you step out of the elevator, when you walk toward her door from twenty feet away. It permeates your clothes, your hair. It permeates every single object, animate or otherwise, that enters or exits the space.

A rent-controlled apartment. Three bedrooms. A foyer. A living room. Thick walls. Ragged parquet floors covered in Turkish rugs. Bookshelves in the foyer. In the bedrooms.

The apartment I grew up in, on Fourth Street and Avenue A. The corner bedroom, formerly mine. From my bed, I'd hear footfalls. My father's heavy barefoot step as he walked down the hall to the bathroom. His soles blackened by the dirty parquet floor.

I haven't spent a night here in over twenty years.)

Earlier. 2011, or so. Before I hired the home health aide.

Smoking.
Eating.
Napping.

Will you bring me some coffee, sweet angel?

Coffee.
Smoking.
A conversation about a helper.

Yes, someone who can help out.
Groceries, other little things.
Nothing major. One day a week.

No. Not a service. I'm not ready for that.
Someone you know, some young person.
Someone interesting.
I-didn't-say-put-an-ad-in-the-NYU-paper-I-don't-want-just-anybody-I-want-someone-you-know-or-who-knows-someone-you-know.
No no no—I-don't-want-a-stranger-in-my-house!

She smokes.

Just a little helper that's all. Can you do that for me? Good.

It's all I need. Between Vince and Marco and Rose and you, I get by.

I'll be just fine.

Michelle. The friend of a friend of a friend. A student, and budding actress. Fifteen an hour.

Blackberries. So good for you. And raspberries.

FAGE yogurt. Those little packages with the honey in them.

Not the low-fat kind. Whole milk is better—if you can find it.

So you're a performer.

How wonderful.

My son works in the theater.

It is a noble profession.

Drinking seltzer.
Smoking.

Swiss cheese.

Coffee, ground, from Porto Rico.

Do you know Porto Rico?

It's on St. Mark's Place.

Porto Rico is a wonderland.

Hershey's Kisses mmm . . . Good stuff.

You'll just have to tell me everything.

All the theater gossip.

I want to know.

Bacon.

Greens, cooked.

Whole Foods?

If you can find me mustard greens . . . I love mustard greens.

Or turnip, or collards.

Greens are important.

Notes on her decline.

It's physical, emotional, and mental.

These being concentric and connected conditions—being progressive, and gradual, until they're not.

The causes multiple, including:

Retirement.

Cancer.

My father's death—they'd been apart for decades but it hit her hard.

Her sedentary existence—inside mostly, in her apartment, in bed.

Cigarettes—a sixty-year habit.

Physical ailments that snowball resulting in:

Less mobility.

More fear.

A smaller world.

A shrinking world.

I'll be just fine.

———

2012—late winter. A few months after I'd hired Michelle to run errands.

She gets ill.

She takes to her bed, even more than usual.

The phone rings.

The phone rings.

Sleeping.

Smoking.

Sleeping.

She pees herself.

Smoking.

Sleeping.

The phone rings.

It rings.

Hello.

Yes? What? I don't know.

I'm just . . .

. . .

Grilled cheese.

And a Hershey bar.

. . .

Smoking.

Eating the chocolate bar I've brought over for her.

…

It just knocked me out.

I slept, for two days straight.

I don't remember a thing.

Dr. Wilson was here this morning, with an assistant.

A bladder infection, she thinks.

A UTI. We'll see what the test says.

. . . I don't know.

. . . Shaky. Weak. Too tired to think.

Okay. Let me see the brochure.

Okay. Set it up. We'll try it. Just for a few days until I get my strength back.

And I make some calls, setting up home care service with what I'm told is a reputable company. Twenty bucks an hour. Maybe twelve of which goes to the aide.

———

Loretta. The home health aide.

A stocky woman in blue scrubs.

In her sixties but looks younger.

Loretta changes the sheets.

Loretta carries the hamper from the bedroom to the kitchen.

She does the laundry.

She goes to the Key Food to get groceries.

She buys butter, eggs, frozen asparagus, and premade pie crust for an asparagus quiche.

I like Loretta.

Loretta is sensible.

Mother smokes.

She drinks her coffee, her seltzer.

She eats asparagus quiche.

Asparagus is full of nutrients.

It's very good for a person.

Like blackberries. And yogurt.

Good stuff.

Hooray.

Smoking.

Reading.

The Weather Channel is on, muted.

Later. She is alone.

Smoking.

Napping.

Reading.

The phone rings.

It's me. She had a cold.

Hello.

Yes.

Fine.

Just here.

Yes, I had a cold. You'd know that if you called.

Uh-huh.

Any hot news around town?

Uh-huh.

Your work is coming along?

Good.

Loretta's coming at three. And Rose tomorrow.

Rose, the masseuse. Seventy-five an hour.

No hot news?

I change the subject, asking about her childhood friend, Bradley.

No, he's not doing good.

I said to him: "Bradley, what are you doing in a hospital in Oxford, Mississippi? What are they going to do with you there? Twist up your gizzards? Go to Memphis at least. Or Atlanta. Somewhere with real doctors."
But he's a homebody, so he won't.
Seventy-five years old, the man has never been on an airplane.

Yes, I did speak with Jack.
I speak with my brother every day.
No, he is not well.
I'm worried about him.
A person who thinks about money always.

Wanted it, spent it. Valued it as a marker of who he was.

And to be without it now . . . it's tough.

It has never been important to me.

But now I'm okay. Now I do have it.

I am protected.

Social Security. Medicare. TIAA-CREF.

I get money for things I barely remember doing.

You need to change the filter.

On the stupidifier.

And clean it.

No not today.

But soon.

When you can.

You're not so busy you can't just drop by and clean a stupidifier.

She eats berries.

She drinks seltzer, and coffee.

She talks on the phone.

Rose comes.

She helps her onto the massage table.

She gives her a massage.

Rose brought me black-eyed peas.

Her mother's recipe. Good stuff.

She's from Tennessee.

Marco. Her good friend. Her "gay son."

Blond-haired, fit. Argentinian. Fifty, but looks younger.

He sits across from her.

He has brought her food, the mail.

They talk. They tease each other. They eat empanadas.

She advises him on all his troubles.

His own mother is thousands of miles away.

They drink coffee. They share dessert.

Good stuff!

Reading.

Smoking.

Napping.

Phone. I ask about Loretta.

Oh yes. My Loretta is good.

She's sensible.

Another week or two of daily help.

Then she could come twice a week through the summer.

We'll see after that, how we continue.

No, not really.

Not back to full strength.

Soon I hope.

I'll keep working.

I'll work with my trainer. Get stronger.

Vince. The trainer. Fifties. Overweight.

Fifty an hour.

In the living room on the chaise longue she smokes.

They chat.

He helps her to the floor, onto a yoga pad.

She lies there as he stretches her.

He manipulates her legs, bringing them toward her chest.

She weebles.

He helps her up.

She smokes.

Do you know what a weeble is?

It's when you're on your back and you weeble back and forth.

Can you weeble?

Vince and me, we weeble.

Weebling is good for me.

I have a very strong back.

Rivka's in Los Angeles.

Edith's away too, down in Texas.

Usually on Sundays they come over, and we have coffee and *croissants*.

But not this week.

I'm just here by my lonesome—reading away.

I'm a happy person.

Are you?

————

Loretta, back on duty.

She changes the sheets.

She makes the quiche.

She fetches my mother's coffee

Along with a bowl of blackberries and several Hershey's Kisses.

Smoking.

Eating.

Drinking coffee from a Mason jar.

Recounting.

Regaling.

For Loretta, who sits in the chair by her bed.

My first husband, Charles, now he liked to drink.

We were at a Christmas party, he and I and Ray and Mara, when he set the ceiling on fire.

I told you about Mara. A beautiful woman.

They ran a printing press in their bathtub—published a Latvian newspaper.

They lived uptown.

We were downtown—on Second Avenue, just off of Fourth.

We used to step over the drunks to get into our apartment.

I put Charles through graduate school.

I was teaching junior high at the time. I supported us for years.

Smoking.

One day 1967 or so Charles he comes home.

"I met someone," he says.

"She's different than you.

Who knows why, but around her, I feel freer.

Is it okay if I see her?

Just for a little while?
Sow the oats?"
I was stunned. Some woman who wore no underwear, he said.
She went around with no underwear.

Smoking.
Dozing.
Her eyes closed, her face at rest.

(Look at her. She's gotten so old.)

(When did this happen? When did she get so old?)

———

Loretta beside her, in the chair, with her hairnet, in her scrubs.

Mississippi—it is the worst place in the world.
From the beginning, I knew I had to get out.
I was a little girl and I dreamed of New York City.
It took a few years, but I did it.

I mean what a place.
The University of Mississippi.
Ole Miss.
All the Miss Americas went there.
All the power people in the state.
Those awful governors and evil senators.
All in the same fraternities.

She smokes.

My daddy was a cotton classer.

He was okay until they drafted him.

They didn't get to him until '43. All the young men were gone by then.

His kind, the old kind, was all that was left.

They sent him off for basic training.

One-hundred-degree weather they made him run.

Shin splints. Sprains. Heat exhaustion.

They pulled all of his teeth—gave him an ill-fitting false set.

He was in tremendous pain.

He didn't make it—they sent him home.

He drank, from morning until night.

That Mason jar full of bourbon and ice rarely left his hand.

It wasn't like today.

No one talked about depression—there was no science for it back then.

He was self-medicating, that's what he was doing.

He died when I was twenty-three.

Loretta goes.

And she is alone.

Smoking.

Napping.

Drinking coffee from her Mason jar.

On the toilet.

On the toilet.
On the toilet.

Hi, pooka.
Not so good.
On and off the throne all night.
Diarrhea.

Notes on shame.

Can you come over here, sweet angel?
I have a task for you.
It's a little embarrassing.
I can't ask other people for this.
I didn't want to ask anyone.
But you're my son.
Can you come over?
Bring your keys.

You startled me.

I help her off the bed and into the chair.

The mattress. I need to turn it.
That's right. One turn, so I have a clean quadrant.
This is an effect of the medication.
I get discharge. And then my bladder, when I laugh—
I do make it to the bathroom.
And I have the towels down, but—

I do fine.

Just one turn . . .

Careful there.

Watch those wires.

See, the phone cord, it's taped in there.

And the lamp. Watch the lamp, it's gonna . . .

I told you!

For God's sake . . .

Look what you did!

I was not being bossy.

Just . . . stop.

Stop stop stop.

For God's sake!

Yes. Finish.

Thank you.

There are light bulbs in the linen closet.

Olga will clean it.

She comes tomorrow.

She'll do it.

Thank you.

Goodbye.

As I go, she lights a cigarette.

Aggghhhh!

She draws the smoke in deep, then releases.

She draws in and closes her eyes.

Back at my own apartment, I strip off my smoke-drenched clothes and step into the shower. I close my eyes and lean my head back, letting the hot water run down my face, my body. Ahhhh!

Notes on the dead.

Anne Nelson, from Georgia. She cleaned my house.
Do you remember her?
A bad cleaning lady, but a good person.

Smoking.

Evan Bernstein.
He ran the agency in Jersey.
Arranged all of our Turkey trips.
Bob heard from Doris, his widow.

Smoking.

Leonard Cross.
Heart attack they think.
A real confusion—they can't find the will.
I'm making phone calls.

Smoking.

Your poor Aunt Dora.
Her brother. Pancreatic cancer.
She's very scared.
That disease—it runs in her family.

Coffee.

Seltzer.

Don Pierce.

He just fell.

Slipped at a construction site.

Fell down into an unfinished basement, cracked his head.

Blood on the brain — they couldn't save him.

We spoke every day.

Matt and Russell.

Pierre's friend Mamadou.

Jerry Portola.

Such a close friend.

He adored you.

Almost thirty years they've been gone, but it feels like it happened yesterday.

These were young men, taken in their prime.

It is a terrible, terrible disease.

The gay men of our household. Her friends and friends of friends, Southerners up from New Orleans, artists and dancers in from Europe and the Middle East. She hosted, she advised, she regaled. She was the queen, stretched out on the chaise longue, holding court in her rhinestones, in her red dress. The queen of the queens.

You know very well I don't see doctors in November.

Between the cancer diagnoses, and your father . . .

These are the way things are.

She smokes.

Your father.

She smokes.

Six years it's been.
I still can't get used to it.
We spoke every day.

(My father. Harold. Her second husband.
Twenty-five years divorced, but they spoke every day.
She would have her packages sent to his address
Because she didn't trust the mailman.
He would come in from New Jersey to deliver them,
Along with cases of seltzer.
He'd move furniture for her
And change the burnt-out light bulbs.

Holidays spent together
Those endless meals
Our awful, inescapable triangle.)

———

A Japanese death poem.

Toshimoto, a samurai, 1331. On the morning of his execution:
From ancient times the saying comes,
"There is no death; there is no life."

Indeed, the skies are cloudless
And the river waters clear.

Basho, a poet, 1694. While dying of a stomach illness:
On a journey, ill:
my dream goes wandering
over withered fields.

———

Notes on e-cigs.

(an idea, a suggestion—for my then unborn daughter's sake, and for hers.)

The science is still not in. Those devices may well pose a health risk.

Smoking.

Nonsense. We air it out all the time.
Olga's always opening windows.

Smoking.
Coffee.

The brochure was useful.
Thank you.

Phone.

That's right. Exploded.

They plugged it into the computer and boom.

It was on the news.

Yes. That thing. USB.

Coffee.

Cigarette—unlit.

Well I do want to see my grandchild.

I fully expect to, on a weekly basis.

Phone.

We went and got one.

Vince wheeled me down to Rivington Street.

I have purchased the starter kit.

Smoking.

Vaping.

Smoking.

Phone.

I did try it.

And it was highly inconvenient.

There's no way to put it down when you're reading.

The contraption is badly designed.

Not to mention the danger.

The FDA, I understand, is considering serious regulation.

Smoking.

Yes, I still have it.

Let me just get things together.

Let me deal with the crises.

Smoking.

They're going to ban them in New York State I hear.

That's right—I read it in the *Journal*.

A ban is a ban. Clearly, they are a health hazard.

Smoking.

Nope. No way. We'll just have to see things differently, now won't we?

Smoking.

Coffee.

Phone.

Bob.

How's that?

Neil Labute—oh come on now. He is the worst.

Bob-you're-talking-nonsense-you're-talking-tripe.

I got to go. My aide's here. Call me later.

Hi, Loretta.

Loretta, who fetches seltzer.

Who makes asparagus quiche.

Delicious.

Good stuff.

Loretta, in her chair, in her blue scrubs, half listening
Half fiddling with her phone.

I was in the tenth grade.
I was on a dirt road, going too fast,
And I flipped the car into a ditch.
The bone broke. It came out from the skin.
Here — on my thigh.
Ten months in traction.
The leg in plaster.
The whole school year, in the hospital, in bed.
My left leg, it's an inch and a half shorter than my right.
It's why I have hip problems.

There she is in her giant bed, with pillows behind her propping her up.

There were visitors.
My mother and father and siblings.
Friends, occasionally.
The nurses.
But mostly I was alone.
I read, constantly.
I took myself away
Escaping, into the ancient world
The classical world.

An Orhan Pamuk novel in her lap.
Along with a murder mystery, which she'll finish later that evening.

That part of the world.

The Near East, Asia Minor.

My absolute favorite.

Stunning.

The stories. The ruins.

Bob and I—we started taking groups there in the nineties. Regal Tours: our side hobby.

Professors mainly. Colleagues of ours from Baruch College. Glorious trips.

That bed of hers. King-sized, at least. With space for visitors, and belongings and much much more.

Istanbul. Antalya. Cappadocia.

It was marvelous.

We used to lay towels out on it and have Chinese food. General Tso's chicken and moo shu pork.

Never retire, Loretta. Retirement is death.

I hate it hate it hate it.

Teaching, it gave me so much pleasure.

It's what I was meant to do.

We used to play Scrabble—we had the deluxe set, with wooden tiles, and a hard plastic board that spun around like a lazy Susan.

People who haven't had cancer,

They don't know what it's like

These treatments, they are heavy.

They say five years clear is the key.

Or maybe ten.

It's been four so far, this go-round.

She was an excellent Scrabble player. So was my dad. We were a family of words.

I have the best doctors.

Oncologist, gastroenterologist, urologist.

Sloan Kettering, it's the only place.

If you ever get cancer, Loretta, find a way to get there.

Don't go in Brooklyn.

When Harold got liver cancer

He saw some doctor in New Jersey.

I said to him: What are you doing out there?

What are you—stupid?

I got him an appointment at Sloan Kettering

But it was too late.

Smoking.

My cancer will come back.

I do everything I can.

I take every precaution, but it's inevitable.

Smoking.

Coffee.

The Weather Channel on, muted.

Daddy wasn't a violent drunk. Except for once, when he hit my sister Charlotte, and he paid dear for that. Mother grabbed a pistol, and took aim at him. She was at the head of the stairs and he was at the foot. Mother was an excellent shot, and she could have killed him, but she changed her mind last minute and shot him in the shoulder. Poor Katherine, on the steps in between, nearly got winged.

Smoking.

Charlotte, she's got cancer too. She is bad off. She blew through her retirement money, has got nothing but Social Security now. She's down in Tennessee, in section 8 housing. I told her, if you want to die, you'll keep seeing that country quack. If you want to get better, you'll come here and stay in my guest room. You'll go to Sloan Kettering and get some real treatment. She'll never do it. She's stuck.

Okay, Loretta. See you Saturday.

Smoking.
Phone.

Loretta made me the nicest quiche.

It's very healthy.
I'm a lucky woman.

Notes on money.
How it is spent. And lost.
Late 2013.

Hello? Pooka.
I'm still waiting on that money from you.
You promised to bring it this week.

I'll be busy from two to four on Wednesday with my masseuse so don't come then but otherwise I'm free.

Two thousand.

Because I need more.

I have to pay people, don't I?

Rose and Vince and Michelle, and Olga the cleaning lady (a hundred bucks every other week).

No, it's been longer than that.

No. No.

Okay. I'll check into it.

She leans down, and opens her drawer.
It's part of the bed, built into the frame.

She leans downs and searches it.
She smokes.
She searches.
She smokes.
Phone.

I'm missing a thousand.

No, I didn't spend it.

It probably fell behind, got stuck deep in the drawer.

I did check.

I did!

Sure, if you want to come take a look, that's okay.

Bring your keys.

In her bedroom, the humidifier hums. The air is stale, unbearable.

I don't know. It's just gone.

These things happen. It's okay.
No one knows about this drawer.
Besides I'm always here.
They don't come in the bedroom without me here. No one does.
Forget it. It's fine. In the grand scheme of things.

It wasn't fine.

The money doesn't matter. I'm a rich woman.

I should have seen it.

It'll be yours anyway, once I'm gone. It all goes to you.
Fine then. Pull the drawer out and we'll take a look.

I pull out the drawer.

Careful with that! My lamp.
My coffee! Watch my coffee.
Right up here. On the bed.

Papers.
Folders.
Small journals.
Cigarette ash—years' worth.
Matches.
Loose change. Foreign and domestic.
Old business cards.
Rubber bands.

Paper clips.

Expired condoms.

A paperback copy of the Kama Sutra.

Throw it away.

That too. In the garbage.

The smoke, the smell of the ashes—I feel ill.

I'm going to hide the money.

In the back, stuffed in here, in this folder, with all the important papers.

That's it. Push it to the back.

It's just gone.

These things happen.

No-no-one-took-it-no-one-could-have-taken-it-it's-just-missing-that's-all.

Can you check the stupidifier?

And that was that. I went home and took a long shower.

I pushed the question out of my mind, and continued as before, bringing her money, two thousand at a time in twenties, whenever she asked for it.

A conversation about water aerobics.

2010 or so—back when it still might have made a difference.

I'll do it another time.

It's too far. And the traffic.

Not in the winter. Maybe I'll go in the spring.

When the weather's better.

I do too.

I leave the house all the time. I walk across the street, sit in the sun.

How would you know my life? How often do you see me? Once a month? Twice a month?

Marco calls me every day.

I'm not saying that I expect that of you, I'm just saying that that's what he does.

If you ever bothered to visit, if you took any interest in my day-to-day existence . . .

I DO TOO.

Oh no. Oh no.

You don't know. There's no such thing as a little cancer.

DIDN'T-YOU-HEAR-ME-I-SAID-THERE-IS-NO-SUCH-THING.

Mythic.

Earlier. Mythic.

How you treat your mother is how you'll treat your wife is how you'll treat every woman in your life.

Mythic.

I have a diary. I write down only the important days. The saddest days, and the happiest ones.

Mythic.

I escaped the South and I have never looked back. I got out.

Uptown. 2013 or so. After a doctor's appointment she's insisted I pick her up from.

She is shaking, crying.

I'm sorry. It ran late.

I'm wasting your time. I'm so sorry.

I'm just dizzy . . . I . . . I . . .

. . .

There's a car service to call . . . I have the number somewhere . . .

. . .

Okay. A taxi. Whatever's fastest.

. . . just get me home

I can't. I can't. I can't.

Shaking. Shaking.

Aggghhhh . . .

I get her into a taxi, and we ride downtown.

She takes my arm, and I help her into the building, the elevator, the apartment—down the hall, into her bedroom, into bed.

Smoking.

Smoking.

Drinking coffee from a Mason jar.

Shaking.

Shaking.

And then she is asleep.

———

(My daughter is asleep, for the moment.

I am at my desk and she is in her bouncy chair beside me.

It is dark out—five-thirty in the morning.

I look at her face, her changing expression.

She is dreaming some sort of baby dream.

It is April 2014 and she is four weeks old.

With my right foot, I gently jostle the chair to keep her down.

Five hundred feet away by the crow's flight is where Mother is: in her bed, in the apartment where I grew up. I have lived in this neighborhood my entire life.

From her bed my mother calls to me.

She gives me money. I go to the candy store around the corner on Avenue A.

I ask for True Blue 100s.

It is the summer of 1978, and I'm nearly seven.

Back then, cigarettes cost a buck a pack.

We're wrestling on the bed.

Her giant scissor legs

Her scar, in the upper thigh

An indentation.

Dinner on her bed. Movies. Even when she was younger, bed was where she was. It was where she wanted to be.

On the bed, both naked, they read.

My father's balls. Enormous.

My mother—the blondish hair between her legs.

A strong fart. They joke about it.

Disgusting.

And then at a certain point they do not like each other.

And he is on the couch.

And she is criticizing him.

This man he is incapable, he is limited, he is broken.

Later she tells me the ways in which he is broken.

His emotional failures.

This is a man who never cries, who does not know HOW to

And when he finally gets a job, after years out of work, she ends it.

He moves out to Queens. I stay with her.

She chooses me.

How you treat your mother is how you'll treat your wife is how you'll treat every woman in your life.

She chose me.)

Look at her. Just look.

I checked my calendar. I went through it day by day.

You get me money once a month.

We have dinner once a month.

Is that all you can manage?

I know you love me, that you're doing your best. I know that these are your emotional limits, but you need to call me.

A person is never too busy for a five-minute call.

She smokes smokes smokes.

You will visit me, right?

You will bring the girl over?

I'm talking later—when leaving the apartment's not so easy.

You absolutely must—this is what is done for a grandmother.

I have all of your books for her.

No not yet.

Once she's four and she can understand them.

You bring her over here and I'll give her every last one.

You bring her over here and—

Oh come on!

You are exaggerating.

The smoke isn't that bad!

It certainly never killed you.

Slam the door on your way out!

Slam.

She is alone.

Bath time.

(My mother bathes.

Naked, with a towel around her, she leaves her room and hobbles down the hall to the bathroom.

She sits on the toilet. The lid is down.

She leaves the towel on the toilet and . . .

Careful, careful, she shifts left onto the gray medical-transfer chair

Then swings her legs over the wall of the tub.

She turns on the shower, which hits her legs.

She takes the washcloth from on top of the fixture and holds it under the water, soaking it. She cleans her underarms. Her chest. Her privates. Loretta handles the places my mother can't quite reach. The feet, the ankles, the back. She leans my mother forward to wash her hair, lathering and rinsing, then taking a towel and drying it vigorously, like my mother once did for me.

Look at her. Her face, it still looks young.

Much younger than her body.

It is a body without shape, without muscle.

Pockmarked with cellulite.

It is a body

Like my infant daughter's body is a body.

My infant daughter's body which is beautiful to me.

I will never bring her to my mother's apartment.

I will never do that to her.)

Bye, Loretta. See you tomorrow.

Loretta robbed my mother. She stole between ten and twenty thousand dollars over the course of a year and a half. The cash I'd brought her, which she'd said she needed, which I thought was going to her employees. But she was paying most of them by check it turned out.

At the DA's office on Centre Street, on the day of the arraignment, we watch hidden-camera footage. In her room, that smoked-filled room, my mother gets out of bed and hobbles to the bathroom. Loretta rises from her chair. She opens the drawer, and in a swift motion, she reaches in and grabs cash.

Agggggh!

She had loved Loretta. She had shared her life with her, had told her everything.

Agggggh!

Notes on consequences. And repercussions.

Fill the stupidifier.
And I need you to bring me the jar of coffee.
And make another potful.
There should be coffee in the big rice tin.

She had misjudged the relationship. She had misunderstood so much. To see the video, to see the robbery, was to peel it all away, to have to face the truth of her situation, to see that I hadn't protected her, that I wasn't able to love her in the way she needed me to. She had depended upon me to be there for her, but I had let her down.

You'll need to check on me more often.
To call me more, in the middle of the week.

Physically, things went from bad to worse. Whereas before she usually made it to the bathroom, now as often as not she simply released.

Her skin started to crack and split. Blisters emerged in terrible spots. Some kind of old age immune disorder—she'll have flareups for the rest of her life.

I don't want to ask the others to do this.

I rely on their kindness, their friendship.

But there's a limit. They are not my children.

Her voice, these days, it's slurred. It's getting hard to understand her on the phone.

I was a very good mother.

The emotional crises, which run deeper. The anxieties, the fears. She lies there, in her bed, on that sunken shit- and pee-stained mattress, that repulsive two-decade-old mattress. "No no no no no" she wails when I suggest changing it. Her face shrivels, her fists shake: "No no no I will not. I will not!"

I never saw you as a child.

I just talked to you like a normal person—like a little adult.

When you needed help getting onto the school bus—

That had never even occurred to me.

And now, it seems, her mind is going. It's not dementia I don't think, not in the clinical sense, but rather some kind of softening, an inability to focus. A vacancy, that I see in her eyes. She can't take things in in the same way, can't quite respond or have any kind of normal conversation—she gets confused too quickly. Even my three-year-old can tell—they'll never know each other, not in any real way.

Here's the thing that gets me: she doesn't read books anymore. She can't retain plot, can't hold it in her head.

Well, no, I didn't say that.
I didn't say that I was well.
If you'd call me, you'd know how I was.

No more books. I didn't expect this. I'd assumed that, at least in this one way, she would always be fully herself.

You didn't think to check in with me?
If you'd checked in, you'd know.
I know I'm such a burden on you.
You and your busy life.
No one's that busy.
As it is you only call out of obligation.
I am an old lady, and will be gone soon.
In the meanwhile, you might try to find some basic human kind-ness and compassion. I worry about the kind of person you are if you're incapable of even that. I wonder how you are as a hus-band, and father. I wonder how you are in your life.

Notes on her death. What it may someday be.

Nighttime. Winter. She is home alone perhaps, in bed.
She attempts to read, but can't focus.
And so she smokes a cigarette before falling asleep.

I love you.
You know that, don't you?

In her sleep perhaps she shits herself.

I may not always like you, but I do love you.

Hi, pooka.

Don't I get a hug?

When she wakes, she tries to get out of bed, to get to the bathroom, but she can't.

(Or does she fall out of the bed? Does she roll to the floor, and break a hip?)

Well, don't I?

She pees herself—again.

She shits herself—again.

Well? Pooka?

She sleeps.

She sleeps.

She sleeps.

It's morning now.

The phone will be ringing.

She won't hear it.

Her body is shutting down.

It's releasing.

It's a smelly mess.

Smoking.

A friend of hers will call me. Edith? Rivka?

"We can't reach your mother. We're worried."

Smoking.

As soon as I open the door, it hits me.

The stench of decay, of human waste—it's all I can do not to puke.

Smoking.
Coffee.
Seltzer.

The police will come, an ambulance, a hearse—however these things are done.

They will wrap her up, and carry her away.

The next day, my work will begin.

An apartment to be cleared out. To be aired out.

The furniture, given to charity—if they'll take it.

The books, drenched in smoke, to be dropped in the dumpster.

The rugs, to be cleaned, sold.

Smoking.
Smoking.
Smoking.
Smoking.
Smoking.

The finances to be sorted.

How dare you?

An envelope explaining everything.

A small inheritance, perhaps.

Journals to read. To burn.

Old correspondence, thrown away.

Love letters from before my birth.

How fucking dare you?

Tax returns.

Photos.

A paperback copy of the Kama Sutra.

I am still here.

The mattress on the sidewalk for Tuesday-morning pickup.

Even through the plastic, it still reeks of shit and pee.

I AM STILL HERE!

———

She smokes.

I smoke.

She drinks coffee.

I drink coffee.

I drink seltzer.

I read.

I talk on the phone.

Round a flame
two tiger moths
race to die.

I'm sorry.

I'm sorry.

Me too. I'm sorry.

…

I'll be gone soon.
You know that, right?

Yes. I know it.

You'll miss me.

…

And you're going to cry for me.

…

You better.

…

You better. If you don't, I'll know it, because I'll be watching.

You'll be dead.

I'll be sitting on my cloud in heaven, peeking down, watching you go about your business.

I'm not sure how I feel about that.

You don't have a choice.

…

What?

Just looking at you. That's all.

…

SON
Do you want to hear about it? Your actual death?

MOTHER
I died?

SON
December 16, 2017.

MOTHER
Oh. Darn.

SON
Yeah. I'm sorry.

MOTHER
What happened?

SON
You fell. And had a stroke. You were on the floor by your bed for a little while—we don't know how long—before you managed to pull the
phone down to yourself and call Marco, around one in the morning.

MOTHER
Who's Marco?

SON
Marco is David. I've been calling him that. To protect him.

MOTHER
That's stupid.

SON
Your left side was nearly frozen. You couldn't really swallow, couldn't get enough nourishment. We gave you crushed ice chips, and tiny sips of water. The new aide, Monica, would mix Ensure and vanilla ice cream and feed it to you with a spoon. She took amazing care of you.

MOTHER
I loved Monica.

SON
She was so good with you. She was able to understand what you needed, which wasn't easy. After the stroke you were very garbled.

MOTHER
Could you understand me?

SON
Sometimes. I got better at it. You found a way to make yourself understood, by all of us.

MOTHER
That's good.

SON
It was day by day. At times we thought you might be swallowing more, getting better. I was exhausted, not sleeping much. There was a day, not

long before the end, when I was totally burnt out. And Monica said to you: "Give Andy a break, let him be with his family." And so I left. But as soon as Monica had left for the day, you had the late-afternoon aide start calling. I said that I'd be there in the morning, but then you had the night aide call, and you made her hold the phone up to your face so you could talk to me. You were begging me to come over.

MOTHER
I wanted to see you. I was dying.

SON
We didn't know how long you would last—we were thinking weeks, or even months. I was trying to pace myself. But yes, it turned out that you were dying. You didn't sleep much that night—it was a final burst of anxiety and fear. We helped you to relax, with medication from the hospice comfort pack. I held your hand. The next day, you started actively dying. Your breathing got fast and shallow—you were gasping for air. That's what happens—I remember it from when Dad died. That night, I stayed over, and David and I switched off being with you in your room. Around eight on Saturday morning I was speaking with Venora, the night aide, telling a story about you, I don't remember what, when we noticed that you'd stopped breathing.

MOTHER
And then?

SON
We hugged—Venora and I, and David. I called the funeral home. In an hour or so, they came to take you away. I dealt with things. You know me—I got right on top of everything. The burial, the clearing out of the apartment, the figuring out of the financial stuff, all of the details.

MOTHER
I bet you did a good job with all that.

SON

I'm good at that kind of stuff.

MOTHER

And the emotional stuff?

SON

I do feel these things. Maybe not in the way you would have wanted me to, but I try.

MOTHER

I wanted you to love me.

SON

What else is all this, but love?

MOTHER

We never had this conversation.

SON

We couldn't. My daughter says you've gone to Die-Land, and that you're not sick there.

MOTHER

She's right. I do feel pretty good.

SON

You look good too. That's a beautiful housecoat.

MOTHER

Why thank you.

Where are we anyway? Where is Die-Land?

SON
Where do you want it to be?

MOTHER
I want it to be in Istanbul.

SON
Istanbul it is.

MOTHER
I'm on a hotel veranda, watching the sun set over the Bosporus.

SON
That sounds beautiful.

MOTHER
Shall we sit here together and enjoy the view?

SON
Yes. Let's.

MOTHER
I'll have a Turkish coffee. And two pieces of baklava.

SON
Coming right up.

MOTHER
And my cigarettes.

SON
Must you?

MOTHER
Yes I must.

SON
Just blow the smoke the other way.

MOTHER
Deal.

SON
It's nice here.

MOTHER
Yes. It is.

[*Pause.*]

SON
Mother. Can I hug you?

MOTHER
May I.

SON
May I hug you?

MOTHER
Yes, you may.

[*They hug.*]

That's tight.

SON
I'm holding on.

MOTHER
I know.

SON
You know, I did cry for you.

MOTHER
When?

SON
At your burial just for a moment, though I was fighting it back then, didn't want to release. It was months later, in a bookstore of all places— the Barnes & Noble on Union Square. I was with Delphie, in the kids' section, and I just lost it—started weeping.

MOTHER
We used to go to Barnes & Noble.

SON
Fifth Avenue and Eighteenth Street. That's where it was back then. I remember it well.

MOTHER
I do too.

SON
I got her D'Aulaires's *Myths*.

MOTHER
That was our favorite.

SON
She loves it too. She loves stories.

MOTHER
We all do. We're a family of stories.

SON
Yes. We are.

[*A shift.*]

SON
Is it time?

MOTHER
Yes. It's time.

SON
…
I love you.

MOTHER
I love you too.

SON
Goodbye, Mom.

MOTHER
Goodbye, Andrew.

SON
Goodbye.